COLLAGE, MONTAGE, ASSEMBLAGE

COLLAGE, MONTAGE, ASSEMBLAGE

History and Contemporary Techniques

Norman Laliberté   Alex Mogelon

An Art Horizons Book

Van Nostrand Reinhold Company
New York Cincinnati London Toronto Melbourne

To Marcia

Library of Congress Catalog Card No. 75-150506

Design Consultant: Milton Glaser
Type set by Lettick Typografic, Inc.
Printed and bound by Toppan Printing Co., Ltd.

Published by Van Nostrand Reinhold Company
A Division of Litton Educational Publishing, Inc.
450 West 33rd Street, New York, N.Y. 10001
Published simultaneously in Canada by
Van Nostrand Reinhold Ltd.

16 15 14 13 12 11 10 9 8 7 6 5 4 3 2 1

Also by the authors:
The Stencil Book (1971)
Twentieth Century Woodcuts (1971)
Drawing with Ink (1970)
Drawing with Pencils (1969)
Silhouettes, Shadows and Cutouts (1968)
Painting with Crayons (1967)
Banners and Hangings by Norman Laliberté
and Sterling McIlhany (1966)
Wooden Images by Norman Laliberté
and Maureen Jones (1966)

Frontispiece:
The Rainbow. Illustration
from *The Yellow
Submarine.* Pen and ink
as well as color pencils
were used to extend the
original illustration.
Patches of shading and
drawing on top of the
original complete the
collage. (Reproduced
courtesy Unicorn
Creations, Inc.)

Opposite Page

Collage by Sauro Bertelli.
Detail from a calendar
produced for Alitalia
Airlines by P.G.B.S.
Advertising, Rome; Sauro
Bertelli, Art Director.
The artist has cleverly
used the collage technique
to represent a famous
landmark. Black and
white magazine cutouts
juxtaposed with solid
sections of color create an
effective and interesting
result.

Contents

Les mots en liberté futuristes by F.T. Marinetti (1909). Experimentation in all directions by artists, architects, musicians, and writers was prevalent during the early 20th century; the wide experimentation in the graphic arts was strongly influenced by the Dada movement. Almost arbitrarily, artists cut out images from magazines and newspapers and pasted them down in various shapes, positions, and patterns producing a type of collage revolutionary for its time.

1.
The Beginning

As periodicals and newspapers became readily available, the art of collage as a folk activity emerged first in Europe and then in America. Its origin can be traced back through the centuries — examples exist of pictures and designs created by pasting together bits and pieces of printed pages to express simple or sentimental compositions and ornamental or decorative themes.

Handmade valentines, paper cutouts and paste-ons, tinsel pictures, scrapbooks (containing product labels, wrappers, pieces of printed advertising, souvenirs, and mementos), screens, vases, and bowls decorated through the use of pasted-on elements — all these are vestiges of collage as an American folk art in the 19th century.

Earlier, Dutch and Flemish artists of the 16th century had produced a number of still-life paintings which deceived the eye with lottery tickets, cards, and torn papers that appeared to be so real that the viewer was tempted to touch them. Raphael Peale, John Peto, and William Harnett were among those artists who continued in this vein in the 1800s.

Finally, during the early 1900s, collage became a form of serious artistic expression as a consequence of the pioneering works of Braque and Picasso. In 1890 Picasso pasted a headline cut from a newspaper onto one of his ink drawings, making it a vital and relevant part of the composition. Almost simultaneously, Georges Braque was experimenting with painted imitations of type and numerals in his compositions, and then began to cut and paste these elements onto the paintings. Very probably the camera contributed to the rapid emergence of the collage as a serious art medium. Picasso, Braque, and other collage artists — Gris, Delaunay, Severini, Boccioni, Arp, Citroën, Ernst, Schwitters — seemed to be saying that the camera had precluded the necessity for creating naturalistic art. What they were attempting was not a denial of real subject matter but, instead, a deep, minutely analytical search to find vital meanings and new values within it.

Quite suddenly, challenging possibilities became evident. No longer could creative urgencies be fulfilled through the techniques of painting on a single plane alone. Space and aspects of the artist's life and personal environment (as reflected through his sensitivities and perceptions) became a cogent part of the composition as materials of many varieties and textures were incorporated and integrated within paintings. The long-standing barriers between painting and sculpture were disintegrating, opening the way to the collage, montage, assemblage, and construction — the new and volatile art forms of an exciting, albeit frightening age.

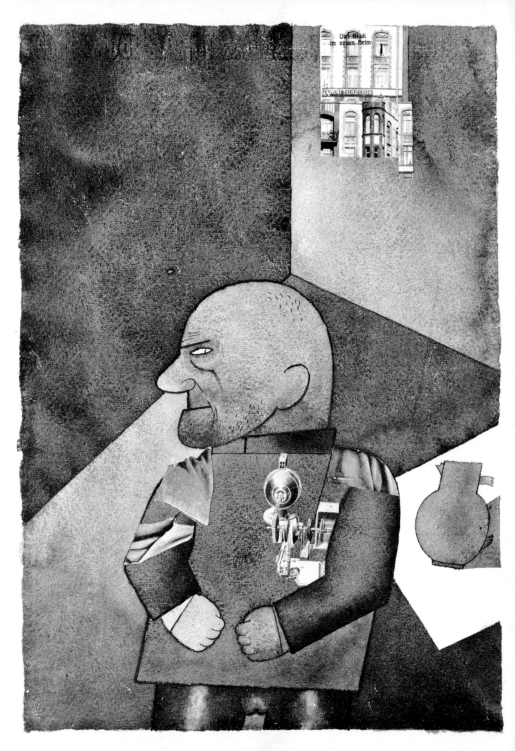

The Engineer Heartfield by George Grosz (1920). A satirical collage in which the artist appears to have cut up and reassembled his own watercolor, adding parts of cities and mechanical objects clipped from magazines to complete the collage. (Reproduced courtesy The Museum of Modern Art, New York. Gift of A. Conger Goodyear.)

Tafel der Greuel by P. M. Bardi (1931). A very tight, busy, and compressed montage of photographs conveying a feeling of the oppressiveness of the city.

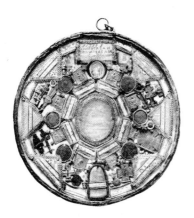

Religious icon, ca. 1900. A number of two-dimensional objects have been assembled to form a large icon.

Musical Forms by Georges Braque (1918). In this
collage the artist has created his subject matter
through pasting up paper forms and painting lines
over the composition. The serious and classical
treatment gives the work the appearance of a
finished painting. (Reproduced courtesy the
Philadelphia Museum of Art, Louise and Walter
Arensberg Collection.)

La Negresse by Henri Matisse (1952). Paper cutouts have been assembled to produce an effective, silhouette-like collage. Matisse's work in collage helped win the medium's serious appraisal and acceptance.

2.
What Does It Mean?
What Does It Say?

"The waste of the world becomes my art," a quotation attributed to Kurt Schwitters in the 1930s, and re-emphasized in contemporary times by Marshall McLuhan, expresses a philosophy basic to the evolution of many kinds of folk art. Not wanting to waste something, people simply put it to use — decorative, artistic or otherwise.

Schwitters, however, was not merely being frugal; he explained his search for new meanings with discarded materials as follows: "I did not understand why one could not use . . . (in the same way one uses color made in a factory) materials such as old tramway and bus tickets, washed up pieces of wood from the seashore, cloak-room numbers, bits of string. . . . From my standpoint, it involved a social attitude and on the artistic level, a personal pleasure. . . ."

The development of the collage embraces, Cubism, Futurism, Dada, Surrealism, and other art movements. The early collage artists searched for what they felt was significant using familiar objects such as bottles, glasses, and guitars and through the positioning of light and shaded areas and the imposition of color limitations. A new burden was placed on the viewer: the assemblage of objects became an image to be read and interpreted. Though objects were usually recognized — a bottle is a bottle and a guitar a guitar — their true significance was not always immediately apparent, and therein lay the real challenge.

The symbols within the collage, montage, assemblage and construction must be interpreted and related to human feelings, experiences, and values in order to evoke individual reaction and understanding on the part of the viewer. Thus the power of a collage composition rests in the use of novel and many times unexpected materials, juxtapositioned so as to elicit psychological response from the viewer.

Work and experimentation in the collage medium by thousands of artists in the first half of the 20th century has contributed to the creation of an environment which encourages the development of art forms and movements embracing the new materials, techniques, and concepts of our time. Though these may at first appear to be strange and are sometimes misunderstood completely, never will they be denied.

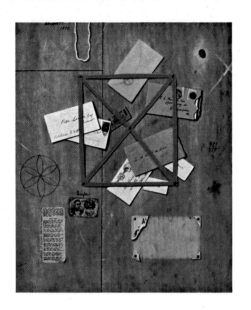

Marmelade von Kirschen.

wird ganz so bereitet wie die Johannis-
Marmelade; nur mit dem Unterschied, daß
anstatt der Johannis Kirschen genommen
werden, wird wohl zu beachten.

*Above, left. The Artist's
Card Rack* by William
Michael Harnett (1879).
This painting is deceiving
because the objects
depicted on the wall
seem to have dimension
and give the appearance
of having been assembled
in collage form.
(Reproduced courtesy The
Metropolitan Museum of
Art, New York.)

*Below, left. Mz 600,
Leiden* by Kurt Schwitters
(1923). Various found
graphic details and
elements were pasted
down, one on top of the
other. Some of the colors
have bled through to add
another dimension to the
collage, while letters,
numbers, and emblems
tend to play against the
flat colored areas.

Right. (Cherry Jam) by
Carl Spitzweg. A very
elegant selection of
materials contributes to
the success of this collage.
The colors are almost
tint-like, and the choice
of type face compliments
the subject matter.

Porträt meines Vaters by
Wilhelm Freddie (1937).
A selection of very
individual objects forms
this collage; yet, either
because of their color or
the background, the
composition has a feeling
of unity.

Left. Still Life and Carafe by Diego Rivera (1914). The artist has given the table, glass, program, pen, and decorative wallpaper a high degree of individuality, and yet each in its own way merges and mingles with the others. Drawing was done over the pasted-up objects to complete the collage.

Right. Antiflache — le bouteille d'Amis del Mondo by Juan Gris (1914). This composition is part painting and part collage; each is so well executed that the viewer finds it difficult to distinguish between the two. The label serves as the point of departure. Note the minimal amount of grays and textures within the collage.

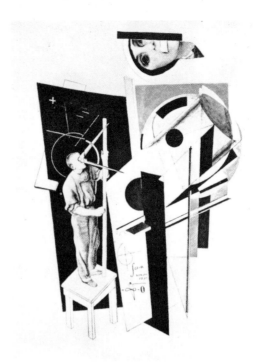

Astronomer at Work by El Lissitzky (1924). The artist has achieved a dynamic composition by the angle in which the various elements have been pasted up. Though flat, they nevertheless emerge highly architectural in concept.

Vase mit Blumen, collage by Freimarken (late 19th century). The artist has created a flower and vase composition by pasting down a selection of postage stamps.

Merz Konstruktion, painted wood, wire, and paper assemblage by Kurt Schwitters. Wood, metal, and other objects have been nailed together in a manner identical to that used in making a paper collage. Objects of varying colors, textures, and ages were selected for their effectiveness. (Reproduced courtesy the Philadelphia Museum of Art, A. E. Gallatin Collection.)

The Guitar by Pablo Picasso (1926). This collage exemplifies Picasso's greatness; playfully combining a leaf, a piece of string, and several quick lines, he has depicted a lyrical guitar and created a highly poetic composition.

Personnage by Jean Dubuffet (1954). Newspaper cuttings and a black ink line around the figure produce a whimsical, puppet-like character.

3.
The Contemporary Collage

The collage, montage, and assemblage of today constitute statements of the human experience in the second half of the 20th century. The kinds of materials employed are limited only by the artist's imagination.

When the concept of collage was new, pieces of printed papers, product wrappers, stamps, wallpaper, ticket stubs, graphics, letters, numerals, and cloth materials were among the principal elements employed. Generally they were unified with work in another medium on a flat background. Contemporary collages and montages embrace almost every substance known to modern man: paper, cardboard, wood, glass, metal, plastic, rubber, canvas, cloth, linoleum, neon, bone, burlap, leather, plaster; natural materials like birchbark, leaves, or butterflies; nylon, and even bread and cookies. Though a good many of these are on a flat surface, almost as many are multi-dimensional, and frequently the nature of the materials used determines the composition's shape.

The techniques employed are as varied and as imaginative as the materials themselves. A number of artists cut up their paintings, rearrange some of the elements, and add objects to create their composition. Others, much in the style of the collage originators, unify and provide an environment for pasted-on found objects by drawing or painting in oils, ink, pencil, pastel, charcoal, or watercolor. In a number of instances, actual items will represent themselves in the composition — buttons will serve as buttons, and medals will be medals. But a series of ticket stubs might serve as the plumage of a bird, or the works of a watch could represent the mechanism of the brain. Imagination and creativity need not have formality, rhyme or reason.

The collage, assemblage, montage, and construction tell many different things about today. Never has art fulfilled this function more forcefully than through the thought-provoking, introspective collage technique. The work entitled

Essex by John Chamberlain is a 9 x 7½ foot junk pile of painted metal pieces that was once a proud automobile. Instinctively, the viewer reviews the car's life span — from production-line birth to pompous showroom preening, from meticulous and proud polishing by an elated owner to the neglect that accompanies deterioration, and, finally, to the wrecker's sledgehammer. One thinks not only of the car, but of the people whose life-style it was intended to project. The parallels between the history of an object and the history of a man inevitably occur to the audience, though not necessarily on a conscious level.

The work of Louise Nevelson represents another kind of modern assemblage artist, one who uses found objects as if they were paints produced by a factory (or very much in the manner described by Schwitters in his comments). Her objects are the odd shapes, forms, and pieces found on the furniture factory floor — wooden balls and discs, posts, dowels, chunks of patterned molding. Usually her composition or construction emerges in a series of boxes or compartments. Sprayed or painted in one color, each box represents a comprehensive study in itself, for the parts and pieces have been assembled with precision, depth, and an overwhelming poetic sculptural ability.

Scenes from life (or still life) are the themes of many modern assemblage and construction artists. These are compelling because many times the viewer has the feeling of being drawn into the scene and the lives of the people the objects served.

Thus a still-life composition like *Kichka's Breakfast* by Daniel Spoerri, which depicts the unfinished breakfast of two individuals, haunts the audience: Who were these people, and where have they gone? We become overly conscious of the objects, for on one hand they represent the living, and yet on the other they suggest the terrible uncertainty of daily life.

Joseph Cornell's work extends the medium into a series of beautiful boxes which, while amidst reality, convey a sense of the universe and a life yet to come. His work embraces many different themes — astrology, medicine, science,

knowledge and learning, nature — arranged in a spirit that evokes nostalgia, romanticism, and, many times, loneliness.

A single chapter, or a single book for that matter, cannot hope to present the work of all the major artists who today work in the collage, montage, assemblage and construction media. What follows are some outstanding examples which say much about the era when they were created and about the direction toward which art in general, and the collage medium in particular, will journey in the future.

The Surge (detail) by Corrado di Marca-Relli, oil and collage on canvas. The artist mounted individual cut pieces of canvas onto another flat canvas surface. He then proceeded to paint on and around the mounted pieces, thus creating a play and a relationship between the background and the pieces that form his composition. (Reproduced courtesy The Cleveland Museum of Art, Contemporary Collection.)

Photo-montage by Ray K. Metzker. The artist has used fragments of various negatives over and over again to create a new entity and entirely new effect. (Reproduced from *The Persistence of Vision*, Horizon Press, New York, in collaboration with The George Eastman House, Rochester, N.Y.)

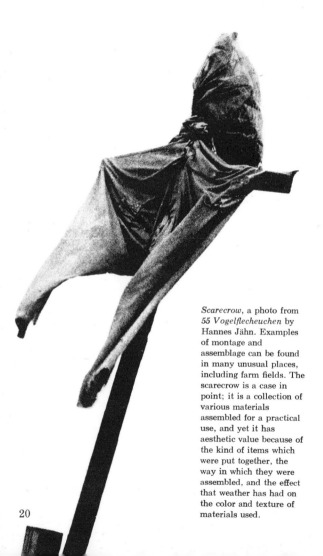

Scarecrow, a photo from *55 Vogelflecheuchen* by Hannes Jähn. Examples of montage and assemblage can be found in many unusual places, including farm fields. The scarecrow is a case in point; it is a collection of various materials assembled for a practical use, and yet it has aesthetic value because of the kind of items which were put together, the way in which they were assembled, and the effect that weather has had on the color and texture of materials used.

Box Collage by Eliot Hubbard. The old tintype photographs, the worn flag which appears to have flown for a century, the clock and its ancient numerals, and the aged quality of the box that holds these objects combine to give the viewer a trip into nostalgia and to create a montage fragment of American history. (Reproduced with the permission of the Botolph Group, Boston.)

Opposite Page

The Legendary Pan Twardowski by Zofia Darowska, cover from Poland Illustrated Magazine No. 8. This exquisite collage has a parchment-like, antique quality, but the contemporary red paste-on tends to pull the composition and the viewer back into the present.

Moon. Assemblage of a wood beam with iron-rimmed wheels and white paint (1960). A strong wooden beam is the central part of this upright assemblage. Four wheels have been nailed on either side to give the assemblage the effect of a motionless locomotive. Moons of white were painted onto the front part of the beam.

Transparencies. Collage and acrylics on canvas by Mansaram Panchal in collaboration with Dr. Marshall McLuhan (1969). This is a new active collage — fragments of tapestry, type, stencil, magazines, and drawings seem to merge with symbols and slogans written in English, Indian, Greek, and Latin to create a universal newspaper composition. (Reproduced courtesy The Museum of Modern Art, New York, Philip C. Johnson Fund.)

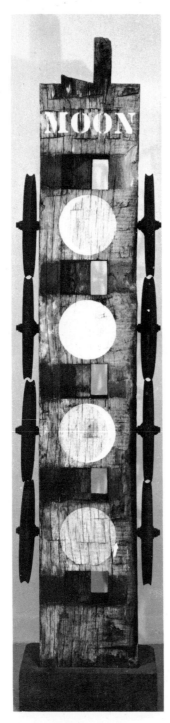

South Carolina Fall by Robert Rauschenberg (1961). In this three-dimensional assemblage, objects have been mounted almost at random, one within another; painting has been added over the objects. Everyday, man-made objects make up this assemblage; they appear ancient because of use, misuse, and altering by present day society. (Courtesy Giuseppe Pauza Si Biurno, Milan. Photograph by Mario Perotti.)

Bed by Robert Rauschenberg (1955). At first glance this work looks like a painting, but upon closer examination the viewer sees the actual fabrics used for the bedspread and pillowcases. Paint has been used heavily on some sections in order to drip onto the neighboring areas; other sections have been left completely unpainted. (Courtesy of Mr. and Mrs. Leo Castelli, Leo Castelli Gallery, New York. Photo by Rudolph Burckhardt.)

Opposite Page

Collage by Fred Otnes.
The artist has created a
collage of American
political figures, past and
present. The viewer also
sees fragments of the
Declaration of
Independence, the Great
Seal of the United States,
the White House, and the
Statue of Liberty. The
composition is an
historical essay, complete
within itself. (Courtesy
Artists Association, New
York.)

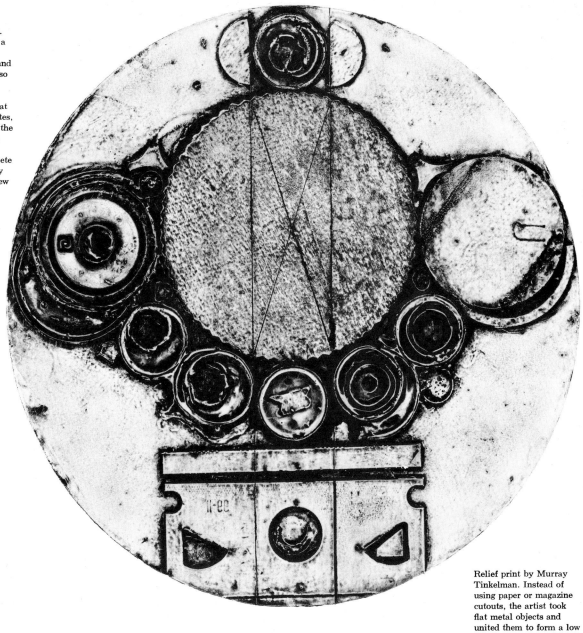

Relief print by Murray
Tinkelman. Instead of
using paper or magazine
cutouts, the artist took
flat metal objects and
united them to form a low
relief composition which
was then inked, and then
a high-contrast circular
print was pulled.

Habitat Group for a Shooting Gallery
by Joseph Cornell (1943). Because they
are encased in the box, the birds become
an intimate, very personal kind of art
within themselves. The smashed glass
— as if a shot has taken place — is
used most effectively in steering the
viewer's eye into the box. (Reproduced
courtesy Irving Blum, Los Angeles.)

Opposite Page

Assemblage by Louise Nevelson. Wooden
objects, shapes, and forms — many of
them found in wood-working factories —
have been arranged one within the other
to create an assemblage of spectacular
proportion. The work is usually painted
in one color, and dimension is added by
light flowing into the room. The viewer's
impression of this assemblage depends
on the proximity and angle at which it is
seen. (Courtesy Pace Gallery, New
York.)

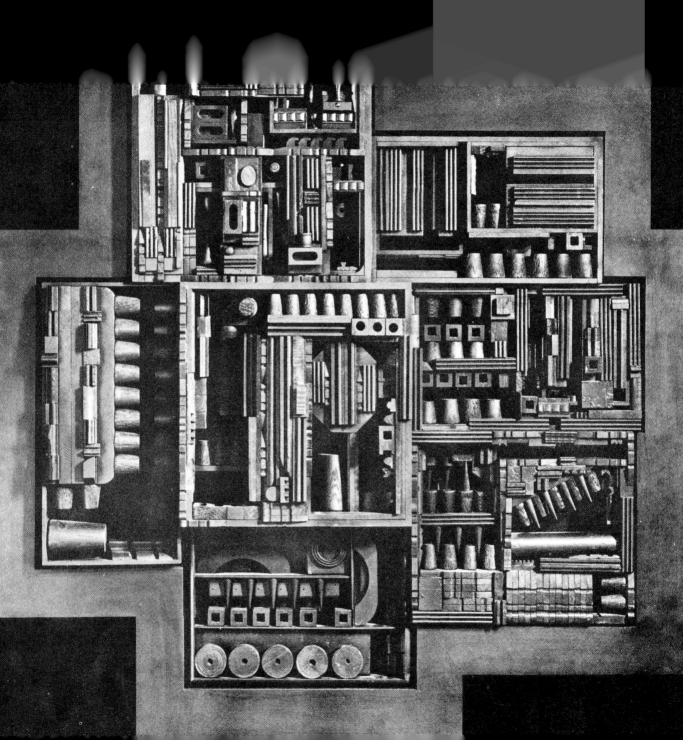

Quantum by Richard J. Chiara. A collage of license plates. The artist has taken a number of license plates of identical thickness and assembled them in vertical, horizontal, overlapping, and angular positions. A thick coating of paint has been applied to suggest that the composition has been intact for many years. As with the Tinkelman low-relief composition (page 27), a print probably could be made from this low-relief montage. (Reproduced by permission of the artist.)

Essex by John Chamberlain (1960). Welded auto metal. Actual parts of an automobile were welded together to form this large, three-dimensional mass. The openness of the metal allows the light to penetrate and illuminate different sections of this assemblage. (Reproduced courtesy The Museum of Modern Art, New York. Gift of Mr. and Mrs. Robert Scull.)

31

Pony Express by Robert Watts (1960-61). An assemblage of wood, steel, polyethylene, brass, glass, a motor, switches and light bulbs. The artist has utilized a small electric motor to activate a brittle construction reflecting elements of America. The outside of a Coca-Cola crate has been covered with pages from a Pony Express account; movement of the horses is the recurring motif of the assemblage, while the flashing lights create an aura of Coney Island. (Courtesy Nationalmuseum, Stockholm.)

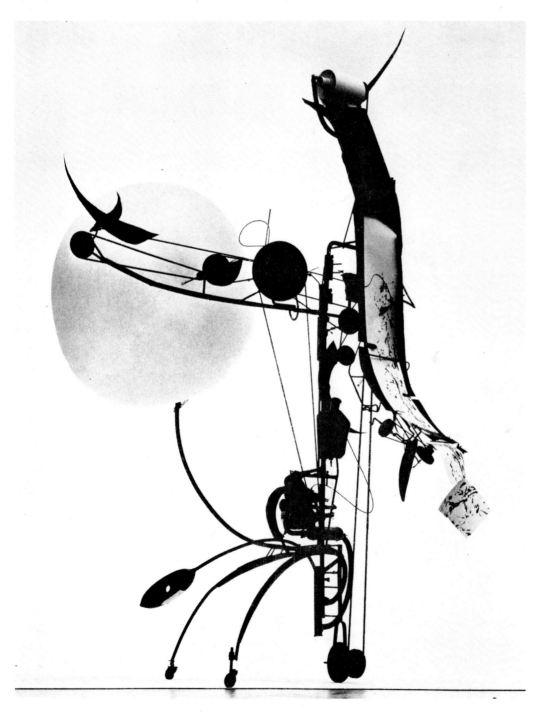

Meta-matic No. 17 by Jean Tinguely. Assemblage of iron. Tinguely's theme is the collaboration of man and machine, suggesting that understanding of the machine could lead man to a better life. Tinguely has been quoted as saying: ''The machine is an instrument that permits me to be poetic . . . if you respect the machine . . . then perhaps you can make a truly joyous (free) man. . . .'' (Courtesy Moderna Museet. Stockholm.)

The Bride Stripped Bare By Her Bachelors, a collage-montage by Marcel Duchamp. This very large, three-dimensional composition has been created from pieces and segments of flat metal, cardboard, and canvas pressed or mounted between two sheets of glass. Some of the objects seem to have been pasted on or etched into the glass itself. The overall effect is one of depth and flotation. The spatial qualities can be altered by rearranging the composition's distance from the wall. The strength of the light is also a significant factor — sometimes objects appear opaque silhouettes but on other occasions they are almost transparent. Moreover, the collage can be viewed from either side, rendering it still more unusual and provocative. (Courtesy of Nationalmuseum, Stockholm.)

Hommage a Pinturicchio
by Romare Bearden
(1969). The artist has
selected paper of various
colors and cut his shapes
quickly with a razor
blade. The choice of color
and sharpness of line
charge this collage with
emotion. (Courtesy
Cordier and Ekstrom,
Inc., New York.
Photograph by Geoffrey
Clements.)

Opposite Page

Fans. Collage designs by Bill Greer. The artist has selected interesting illustrations from magazines and periodicals to cover old-fashioned advertising fans, Although the shape of each fan is identical, the choice of images and their placement produce different and interesting effects.

Collage cover by Eric Von Schmidt for *Notes of a Native Son* by James Baldwin (Bantam Books, Inc.). The collage medium is a most effective way of rendering a book cover. Here the artist has used subtle overlays of fabric to create a varied background for dramatic figures in black and red.

Collage cover by Arthur Shilstone for a publication of Abercrombie and Fitch Co., New York. At first look, this collage appears to be a watercolor. Hundreds of little pieces of thin, transparent paper have been combined and glued to give a soft and subtle effect. The gradual merging of the colors gives the composition a highly luminous quality.

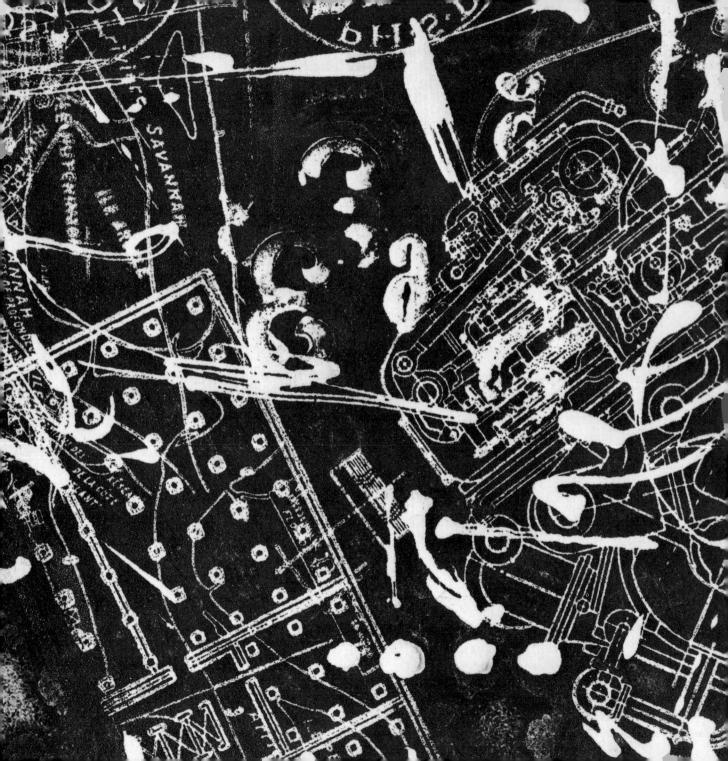

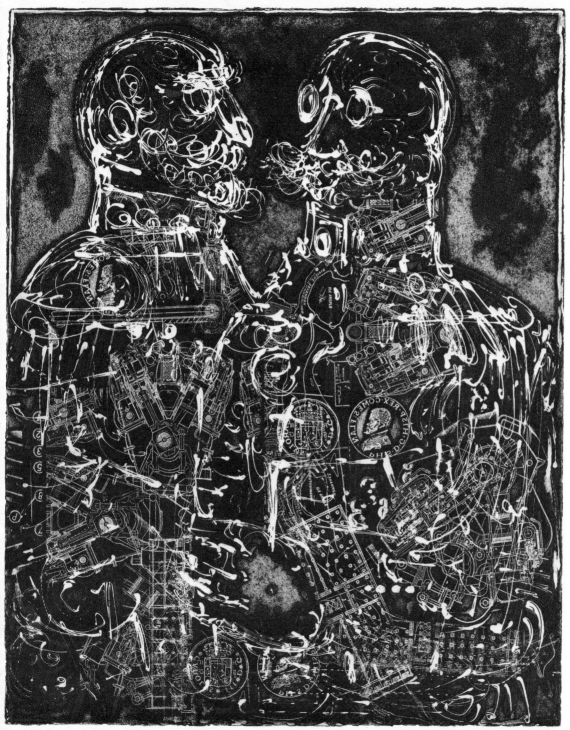

Opposite Page

Detail from *Two Generals,* a montage drawing (seen in full at left) by Misch Kohn. The artist employs X-ray, electronic, computer, and old coin components and symbols to form the mass of his two figures, giving a photographic quality to this montage. Lines were etched around the objects to unify the composition. Though the work resembles a drawing, a closer look reveals the clever use of photonegative collage techniques.

Following Pages

Shouting General by Enrico Baj, 1960. Oil on canvas with brocade, hemp, clock dials, medals, cartridge belt, rope, embroidery, and water flask. The large figure has been painted on the canvas and adorned with large and small objects representing medals, epaulets, and the decor of war. (Reproduced countesy Galleria Schwarz, Milan.)

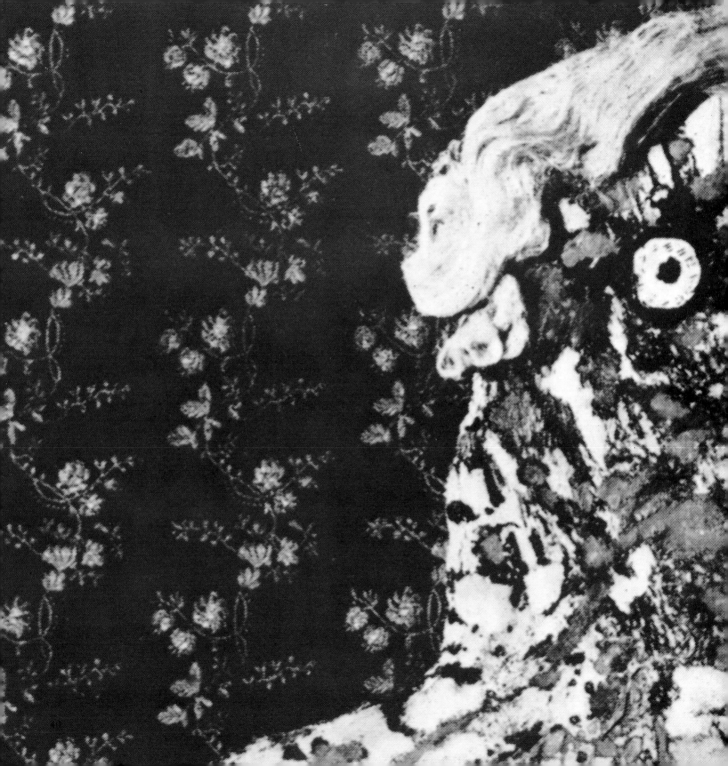

Right. *Stravinsky Collage* by Larry Rivers (1966). Collage with pencil, pastel, and crayon. Parts of magazines, newspapers, and music books have been pasted down to form a Stravinsky portrait. Pencil and pastels have been added to emphasize areas or to delineate elements of the composition. (Reproduced courtesy Svensk-Franska Kongstgalleriet, Stockholm.)

Left. *Excelsior* by Alfonso Ossorio (1960). An assortment of miscellaneous objects and vitreous materials together with the artist's own illustrations have been mounted on a six-foot tall wooden board to form an effective collage. (Reproduced courtesy Betty Parsons Gallery, New York.)

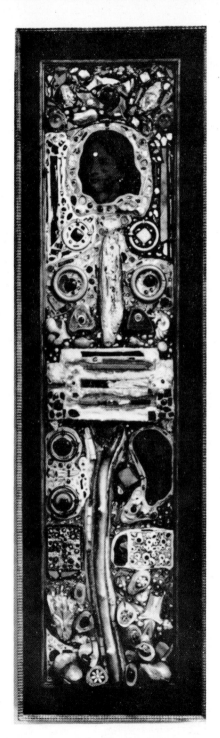

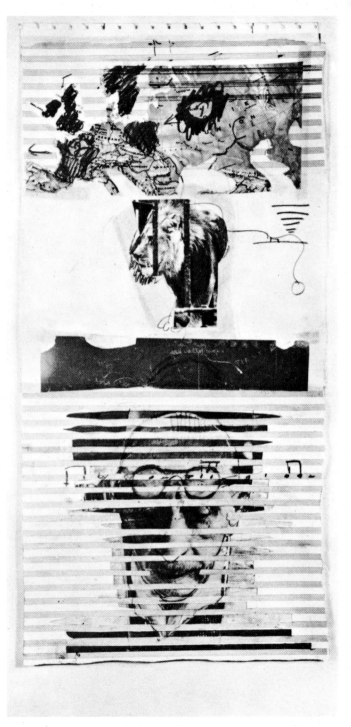

Guanajuato by Aaron Siskind (1955). The outdoor wall advertisement ravaged by the elements is like a "time" collage. Weather has worn and torn the original sign, revealing elements of older print beneath it. These merge with the new to convey an almost wistful feeling of the impermanence of the present. (Reproduced courtesy of the artist.)

43

No. 6 — 1965 by Richard Lindner.
Watercolor, ballpoint pen, pencil, and
collage. The artist's watercolor covers
most of the collage area; bits and pieces
of magazines and newspapers have been
incorporated within some parts of the
painting. The added elements have been
painted over. (Reproduced courtesy of
Cordier and Ekstrom, Inc., New York.)

Head. Collage by Bill Greer. The artist
rendered two different drawings with ink
and brush on white paper, then tore
them at different positions. By repasting
them, a fragmented quality has been
achieved, much like Siskind's time-worn
sign on pages 40 and 41.

Untitled. Assemblage of steel, canvas, cloth, and wire by Lee Bontecou (1960). This huge construction (5 by 6 feet) is 20 inches in depth. The form of the composition is made of steel; wire has been attached to vary its depth. Canvas and cloth of different colors and thicknesses were attached around the wire creating levels and openings of varying sizes. The surface of the assemblage resembles the terrain of the earth as seen from the air, and as the viewer walks around the construction, different impressions evolve. (Collection of Mr. and Mrs. Robert C. Scull, Great Neck, New York.)

Opposite Page

Collage by Mimmo Rotella (1960). It appears that the artist has ripped apart a series of billboards or posters and repasted them to form his own composition. In Siskind's collage (page 43) the ravages of time produced the result; in this case, the arrangement was controlled by the artist. (Reproduced courtesy of Gebrauchsgraphik International Advertising Art.)

Neptune's Casket. A multi-color collage print by Myril Adler. The techniques used in creating this composition are demonstrated in the chapter beginning on page 55.

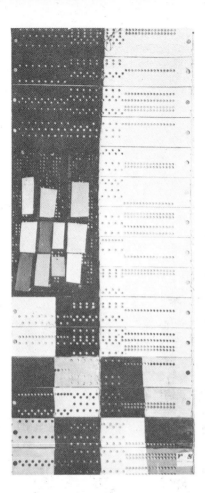

Collage by Vera Spencer. Found materials were mounted in a very formal way to create a severe and orderly collage. The even position of the holes gives the composition a regimented, electronic-age appearance. (Reproduced courtesy Rose Fried Gallery, New York.)

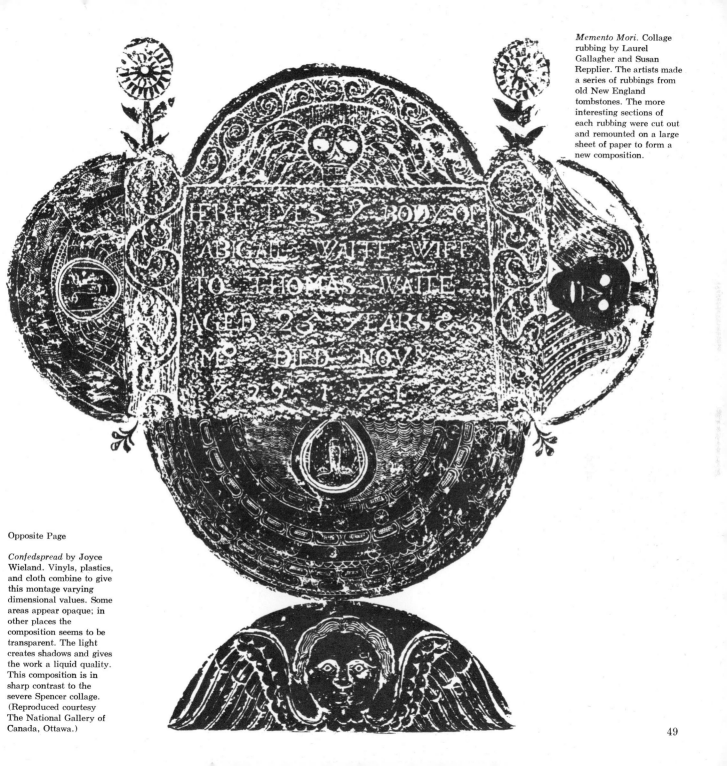

Memento Mori. Collage rubbing by Laurel Gallagher and Susan Repplier. The artists made a series of rubbings from old New England tombstones. The more interesting sections of each rubbing were cut out and remounted on a large sheet of paper to form a new composition.

Opposite Page

Confedspread by Joyce Wieland. Vinyls, plastics, and cloth combine to give this montage varying dimensional values. Some areas appear opaque; in other places the composition seems to be transparent. The light creates shadows and gives the work a liquid quality. This composition is in sharp contrast to the severe Spencer collage. (Reproduced courtesy The National Gallery of Canada, Ottawa.)

49

Knight by Myril Adler.
An assemblage of found
metal objects which have
been inked separately and
put through an etching
press to produce a
fascinating print.

4.
Demonstrations

Collage and assemblage techniques are used with a high degree of imagination and skill by Myril Adler to create multi-colored prints of great strength and sensitivity.

Mrs. Adler, whose watercolors, oils, and prints have been exhibited throughout the United States and in Europe, uses the collage concept in work that takes two different directions. Her prints are composed of segments and pieces of metal, wire, cardboard, screening and other low-relief objects, both found and manufactured, which are inked and run through an etching press to produce a print. This section will demonstrate the techniques she employs in creating her prints.

Once a print has been completed, Mrs. Adler will tear up or cut out of it certain graphic elements which become central themes in the creation of entirely new and individual works of art involving a multitude of materials including oil,

acrylics, watercolor, Cellotex, insulation board, latex, and almost any useful material that comes to hand. In effect she creates (through the print medium) her own "found" objects that serve to stimulate and inspire the creation of entirely new compositions that have a mysterious and unique quality about them.

"My collages grow from different roots," Myril Adler says, "a personal vocabulary of texture and forms through the imprinting of rag papers with intaglio etching.

"I am stimulated by the brilliance of oil-based printer's inks which become fused with the paper through the great pressure of the etching press, and the endless variables of textured surface.

"In searching for an archetypal imagery I have evolved certain shapes, color combinations, and surfaces in which fragments taunt and intrigue me with their own possibilities. Torn, cut,

painted into, pasted on flat, raised or carved surfaces, an endless variety of statements develop. In combination with dyes, inks, acrylic or oil paints the widest range of color hue and intensity becomes possible, from the pristine quality of the untreated paper to the deepest pool of multi-printed dark."

This chapter demonstrates some of Myril Adler's basic collage techniques in creating multi-color prints.

Though the print-making techniques outlined are important, what is significant to the student of collage, montage and assemblage is Mrs. Adler's creative use of self-made shapes and found objects and materials to produce prints that are imaginative compositions within themselves. At the same time, graphic elements within these prints are of such strength and stature that they can be torn or ripped from their original environment and used as "found" objects in the creation of new compositions.

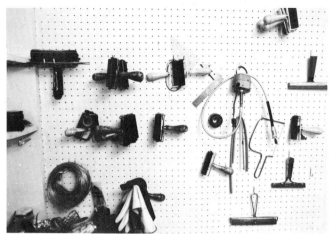

1. Some of the tools used in printmaking include rollers of varying size, hand drills, wire and metal instruments.

2. More working tools . . . brushes of different bristle quality, metal cutouts, shapes and forms, pins and nails.

3. The principal background of the composition is an intaglio zinc or copper plate that has been distressed and pockmarked by acid and with various power tools. Ink is being applied below the original level to cover the various surfaces and characteristics of the individual crevices and holes.

4. The excess ink — or ink that has remained on the flat plate surface — is cleaned off with a cloth.

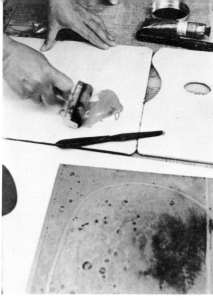

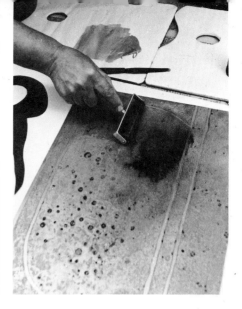

5.   Many varieties of inks are used in a multitude of colors.

6.   The ink is rolled back and forth on a paper before application to the plate in order to regulate its density and to assure that it will spread evenly.

7.   The ink is applied to the surface of the plate. The holes and crevices (page 50) were inked in a different color.

8.   The form or shape — cut from a sheet of lithograph plating — is inked separately in its own color.

9.   The wire — a found object in this case — is inked.

10.   The two inked elements are positioned on the background intaglio plate.

11. The entire composition is now placed on the etching press.

12. A sheet of paper is placed over the composition. Experiments should be made with papers of different textures, qualities, and colors to produce prints that vary and have individual characteristics.

13. A blanket is placed over the paper before rolling the composition through the press.

14. Printing the composition. (The completed work appears in page 50). The gauge of metal from which the figure was cut and the thickness of the wire (in addition to their individual color) leave an effective impression on the print, delineating and emphasizing elements within the composition; this could not be achieved if all the elements were done on a single surface plate. On the intaglio etching portion of the composition, the pressure of the press has fused the ink from the various surfaces with the paper to form an infinite variety of textures and rich, intense coloration.

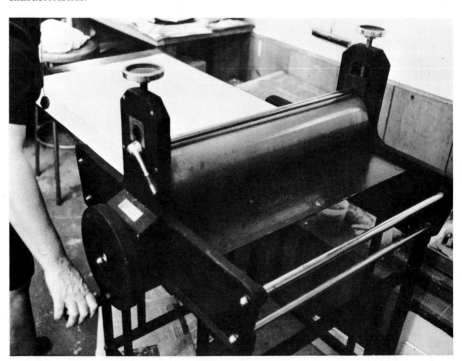

1. A collection of hinges, lock and key hardware, metal and craft objects — some manufactured, others found — all of which can be used in collages for low-relief printmaking.

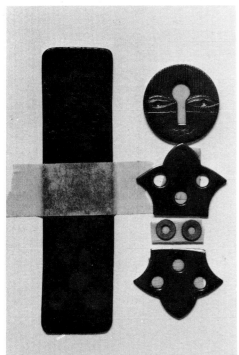

2 and 3. Selections of flat found and manufactured metal objects can be arranged in collage compositions and printed in one or more colors. As stated previously, papers of varying textures, weights, and colors should be tried out in making prints of this kind. Both hardware stores and junk shops contain a world of objects from which a variety of colorful, low-relief collage prints can be created.

Papalota. A collage print by Myril Adler.

The isolated elements used in the
composition. The background tablet
emerges from a distressed zinc plate
which is treated in the intaglio technique.
The hands and orb were cut from
lithographic zinc sheeting. Because each
element is a separate entity, the artist
has a great deal of flexibility in creating
the composition and is assured of
remarkable color clarity. These elements
can be interchanged, resulting in endless
variety.

Photographed on this page are various elements which Myril Adler has found or created to produce her collage technique color prints. Some of the basic background sheets are power-tool and acid distressed to be printed in the intaglio method. The shapes and forms were generally cut or fashioned from lithographic plate sheeting, and thus they have their own unique printing qualities. As mentioned, there is great flexibility or variety of choice, simply because the elements are individual and therefore interchangeable. The prints produced in this manner are imaginative works of art in themselves. Some of the graphic elements serve to act as "found" objects and, when torn or cut from the printed work, are the catalysts and principal motifs in new works of art in still another medium.

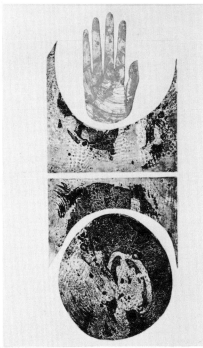

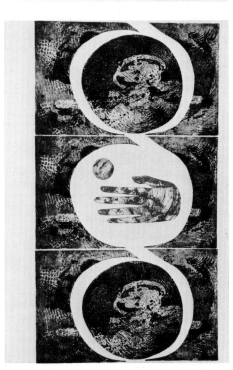

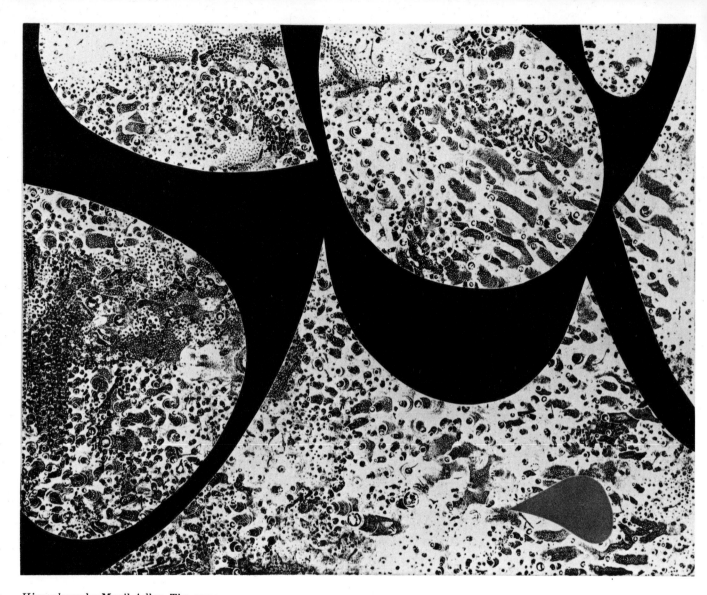

Hierophany by Myril Adler. The same
flat objects can be repositioned and inked
in varying colors to produce prints that
differ from each other but still possess
the identical overall elements.

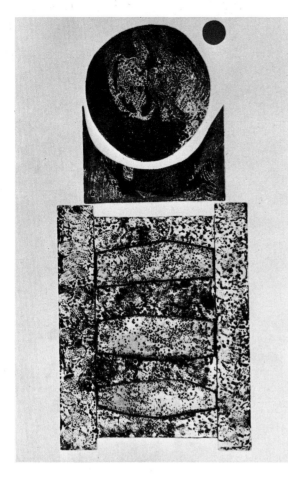

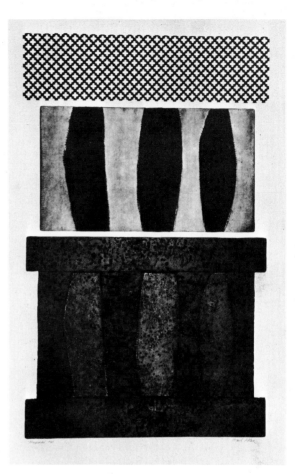

Elements for the collage print entitled
Jacob's Ladder by Myril Adler.

Elements for Myril Adler's collage
composition *Thresholds*.
The artist has created a complete
vocabulary of shapes and objects, large
and small, found and manufactured, from
which she can virtually speak the
language of collage. Materials range
from cardboard and heavy paper packing
to metal sheeting and screening. Not only
is shape important, but the thickness of
the object and its texture all help to
determine the result in the quality and
individual personality of the completed
print. Perhaps the greatest virtue of the
vocabulary is the flexibility or
spontaneous freedom which it allows the
artist in creating collage compositions
for low-relief printing.

Following Pages

The Wiesbaden Special
by Norman Laliberté.
Pieces of gift wrapping
paper, old maps, and
portions of postage stamps
were stapled onto a sheet
of cardboard. A felt nib
pen delineated the
locomotive, and watercolor
was added to give it
shape.

Greek Coin. Part of the
coin illustration was cut
out and pasted onto
paper. The illustration
was extended and
continued with fine brush
and ink drawing. Washes
were applied within the
drawing itself.

5.
Collages by Norman Laliberté

Norman Laliberté works in a number of media, including oil crayon, cloth, ink, pencil, wood, pastel, charcoal, and chalk. Many of his compositions are created through still another form of artistic expression — collage — using the most economical materials of all: found graphic images and objects.

Laliberté's studio is a virtual storehouse of materials collected at random but kept for the purpose of contributing towards, and frequently suggesting, the nature of work in the collage medium.

The range of items is astounding in scope, yet most of these graphic objects and images are readily available a dozen times a day throughout the year. These include old catalogs and periodicals, foreign newspapers, posters, materials received in the mail (advertisements for books or seeds), cigar bands, stamps, candy wrappers, packaging insignia, gift wraps, gum cards, holiday seals, old snapshots, valentines and Christmas cards, menus, banana stickers, theatre stubs, bus transfers . . . the list is endless.

Of greater significance than sheer variety is the way in which these materials are put to use in the collage medium. There appears to be a natural flow or relationship between the nature of the material and its place within the work itself. It is more than a simple process of building a picture by the use of shapes or forms alone. Each found object, in addition to shape and color, has a visual personality or characteristic of its own, and this is what it will contribute to the success of the overall collage.

For instance, a butterfly cut from a piece of gift wrap does not necessarily represent a beautiful insect alone; instead it may serve as the crowning touch to figures executed in ink or crayon indicating royalty or an air of exaltation. Similarly, a ticket or a transfer may serve as the body of a vehicle of transport or of motion. It is not the form of the object alone that places it in the collage (after all, isn't a chocolate bar wrapper oblong in shape, too?) but rather its purpose in real life.

These, of course, are simplifications to facilitate explanation. Frequently, the reasons for the use of certain materials within a Laliberté collage are not as obvious. They involve (many times in a subtle way) moods of romanticism, sentimentality or nostalgia, or give the composition an atmosphere or a spirit important to the strength of the subject matter. Position and juxtaposition are always significant, too, because these can provide elements of surprise, shock, joviality, or amusement.

The pasted-on graphic image or object is not complete in itself. Laliberté will draw or paint over it, incise, scratch, or cut into it, thus incorporating or uniting it with the rest of the composition which, in most instances, is done in a composition of crayon, ink, pencil, pentel pen or watercolor media.

Born in the United States of French Canadian parentage, Laliberté, after a brief career as a photographer and service in the U.S. Army, found himself embarking on a career as an artist at the Montreal Museum of Fine Arts at the age of 20. He continued his studies at Cranbrook Academy and at the Illinois Institute of Technology, where he received an M.S. degree. He has taught art in a number of schools, including the Rhode Island School of Design.

Laliberté's work is in many ways deceptive or childlike, but is never childish, for the images and symbols he creates merge and mingle with complexity and sophistication. Whether his theme is the Bible, mythology, history, or folklore, there is an immediacy about his work that projects the sensation that time itself has been dissolved.

The collage medium — which provides for the use and inclusion of everyday graphic and natural materials in Laliberté's work — adds to this feeling, for these (even if in the composition they represent the crown of an ancient king) are, after all, products of "now" and this generation.

This chapter illustrates a number of Laliberté's collage compositions and examines some of the techniques he has employed in creating them.

Altar Piece. Pieces of black paper and sections of old postcards were cut out and pasted together, then photostatted. The fine white lines were scratched into the photostat with a sharp instrument.

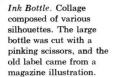

Ink Bottle. Collage composed of various silhouettes. The large bottle was cut with a pinking scissors, and the old label came from a magazine illustration.

Opposite Page

Dark Haired Girl. The principal element of this collage came from a postcard. A frame was added around the figure, and color pencil was used for the drawing of the head and for providing additional detail.

Pages 68 and 69

Home Sweet Home. A number of old Currier and Ives calendar prints were used to form the basic elements of this collage. Items like the house, the little girl, and the dog were cut out from the prints and pasted onto the paper. Parts of trees were cut and reassembled to form a new tree. The background and foreground were drawn and colored with pencils and pastels, while overall black pencil lines were added to unify and complete the composition.

The Magical Rose.
Illustrations for a poem by
Joseph Pintauro. Various
pieces from newspaper
advertisements were used
to make this collage. The
poem around the figure is
in Prestype.

Opposite Page

Eastern Rites. Bits and
pieces from a Chinese
newspaper were pasted
together almost
arbitrarily. Fine brush
and ink, loose and free
calligraphic lines were
added around the pieces
to unify the composition.

Page 72

Soldiers. Kraft paper
pieces form a head, the
body, and the hat; black
ink and brush lines were
applied over these to form
a drawing. Shadows and
textures were achieved
by drawing over the kraft
paper and ink lines with
white chalk.

Page 73

Winter Scene. In this
instance, the collage began
with a basic brush and
ink drawing. Newspaper
pieces form the body of
the girl, while gummed
Christmas seals affixed
around the head and
light gray and pink
Zipatone applied over
the newspaper complete
the composition.

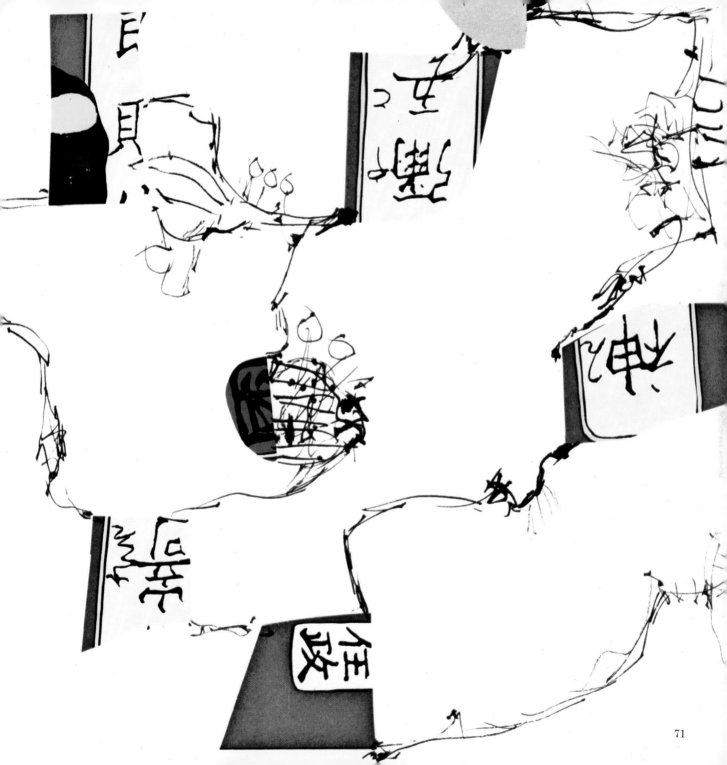

F-100

the ma
36.8:C 7(

82

83

PER DRY DEODOR
NET WT 5 OZS

84

42041

ation 1.50

RESERVED
ES. INC. 1966
GRAPHED IN CANADA

2

Before Corte
Middle Ame
Year 1200, a

RY-M
488

is 500
day!

7th

89

90

91

OCT
28
1967

10578

19

RE 3
VAR

REG.
$1.29

88

28 29

3066 40
LOT NO   SIZE

1: 6
lude
efer

168. 9 p.

12 p.

IT

Page 11

92

8¢

98

93

94

95

1.
2.

12¢

51L.
ary 1,
ploym
L 7.61:

C-5 Galaxy—

LALIBERTE

254

196716

35

PRIJS 34 CENT

96

97

98

99

ent of Doc
20402

1969
May 3

Model AGFE
11,500 BTU
115V/12 An

exact measured
alrod @ surface
ght, clock, min-
ice outlet, stor-

101

102

.... .08
.... .16
.... .24
.... .32
.... .40
.... .48

10,

103

1968

104

No. 11
0, 1969

10

CLASS

E 327
SEASON MODEL

PAGE
8

3.

6L
7L
8L

108

PAID
mit No.
ORK, PA.

20402
ESS

DAYS

109

May 30, 1
No

110

Preceding Pages

Number Graph. Numbers found on various graphic elements (stamps, labels, price tags, cigar bands, menus, cleaners' tickets, theater stubs) were pasted at random onto a piece of regular graph paper within the grid system to form an unusual and effective collage.

Flowering Madonna. A postcard was pasted in the middle of a piece of paper, and various decorative elements were placed around it. Watercolor was brushed into parts of the drawing, while the Madonna's dress was completed with color pencils. Flower decals add embellishment to the composition.

Pages 78 and 79

Uncle Nunzio. Collage illustration for a poem by J. P. Uncle and the smoke from his cigar have been cut from paper doilies; a cigar band is used to depict the cigar. (Reproduced courtesy of Harper and Row.)